Whose H...

Contents

Who Has Hooves?	2
The Horse Family	4
Hooves with Two Toes	6
Hooves with Three Toes	8
Hooves with Four Toes	10
Hooves in Action	12
Fabulous Feet	14
Index	16

Who Has Hooves?

Some animals have paws or claws.
Some animals have hooves.
A hoof is a hard foot.

Look at these animals.
Do you think they
all have hooves?

The Horse Family

Horses have hooves. So do donkeys and zebras, which are related to horses.

Donkey

Zebra

Do You Know?

Some horses wear shoes to protect their hooves.

Hooves with Two Toes

Some animals have hooves with more than one part. The parts are called toes. Look at the giraffe's hoof. It has two toes.

Do You Know?

The scientific name for animals with hooves is *ungulates*.

6

Springbok

Goat

All these animals have hooves with two toes.

Cow

Sheep

Hooves with Three Toes

Did you know that rhinoceroses have hooves? Rhinos' hooves have three toes.

Do You Know?

All animals with horns have hooves.

Hooves with Four Toes

Look at the hippo's hoof.

It has four toes.

They are hard and strong.

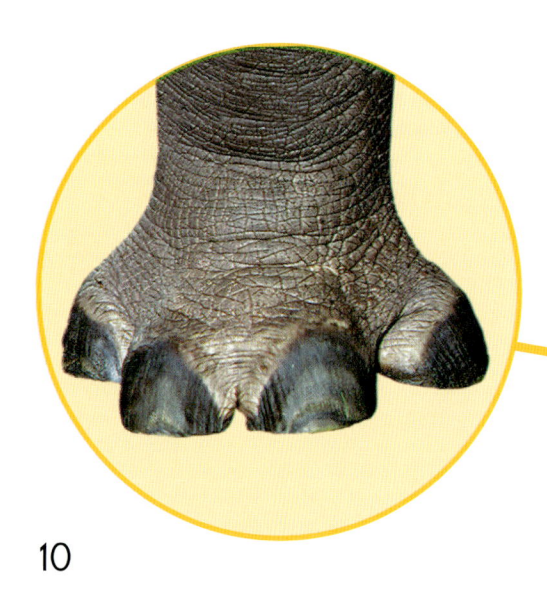

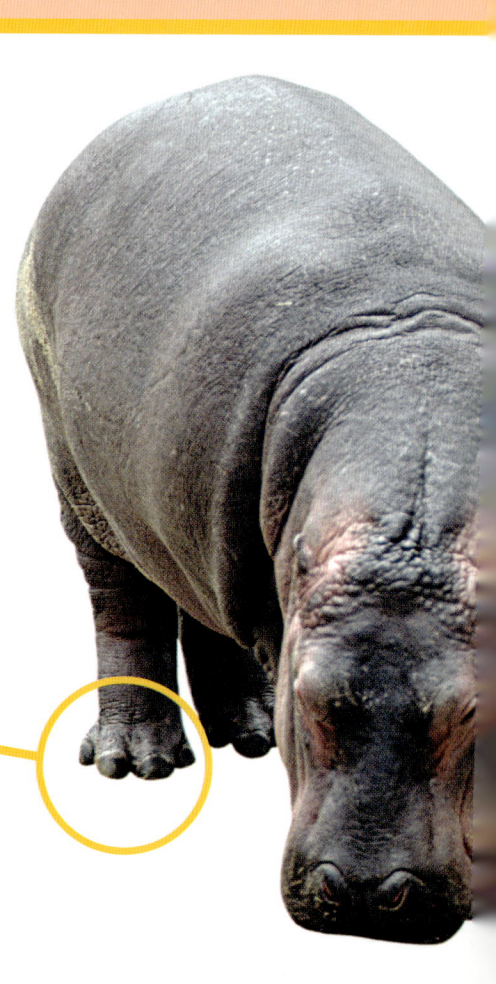

Do You Know?

Animals in the pig family also have hooves with four toes. They walk on the front two toes.

Warthog

Hooves in Action

Hooves are hard and strong. They are good for walking and running. What else can animals do with their hooves?

Goat

Zebras

Deer

Elk

13

Fabulous Feet

There are many more kinds of animal feet. Look at these!

A seal has flippers.

A lion has pa

This lizard has sticky pads on its feet.

A sloth has claws.

A frog has webbed feet.

15

Index

claws	2–3, 15
donkeys	4–5
giraffe	6
hippopotamuses	10
horses	4–5
paws	2–3, 14–15
rhinoceroses	8–9
toes	6–11
zebras	4–5